JESUS IS ENOUGH

Jesus is Enough

Copyright © 2020 by Eric Gilmour

All rights reserved solely by the author. The author guarantees all contents are original and do not infringe upon the legal rights of any other person or work. No part of this book may be reproduced in any form without the permission of the author.

Scripture quotations taken from the New American Standard Bible® (NASB), Copyright © 1960, 1962, 1963, 1968, 1971, 1972, 1973, 1975, 1977, 1995 by The Lockman Foundation Used by permission. www.Lockman.org

Scripture quotations marked (KJV) are from The Authorized (King James) Version. Rights in the Authorized Version in the United Kingdom are vested in the Crown. Reproduced by permission of the Crown's patentee, Cambridge University Press

ISBN-13: 9781711795027

A Publication of *Tall Pine Books*

|| tallpinebooks.com

*Cover art illustration by Brit Richards

JESUS IS ENOUGH

ERIC GILMOUR

Tall Pine

CONTENTS

Foreword — vii
Introduction — xi

1. Jesus is Enough — 1
2. Jesus is Enough: Part Two — 9
3. Jesus our King — 23
4. How to Experience Jesus as Enough — 33
5. How To Experience Jesus As Enough: Part Two — 41
6. Jesus Is Our One Necessity — 51
7. Loving Jesus — 63
8. Loving Jesus: Part Two — 71
9. A Call To Love Him — 81
10. Jesus Alone: A Word from Eric's Wife — 91

Meet the Author — 101
Also by Eric — 103
Maxims — 105
Notes — 119

FOREWORD

Jesus is everything.

He is the Father's only sermon.

He is Heaven's light, as there is no sun there.

He is the object of Heaven's affection. Heaven's saintly and angelic choirs sing of Him eternally.

He is the source of their lyrics, the means by which they sing and the object of their adoration. His Spirit makes the songs audible and gives them breath.

There is no temple in Heaven because Jesus is the temple.

He is both the temple and the One who fills it.

He is the heart and the will of the Father, the Son of His love.

He is all in all there.

May He be all in all in our hearts.

Hebrews tells us that Jesus is the actual speaking of the Father. Our Father will forever speak one thing: "This is My Son." Why would He only say this one thing? The answer is so simple that it sends a dart of love through the deepest recesses of our spirits. Friend, in saying "Jesus," He has spoken everything. There is simply nothing left to say. The scriptures tell us that Jesus descended and ascended to "fill all things." Again, the scripture says, "in Him all things consist." This language is majestic and beyond wise! He has filled all, contains all, and is all in all. There is now nowhere else to look. There is no other place to go. There is no other vision worth having. There is nothing left to see. Jesus is the source, the means and the goal. Jesus is not a mere bridge to a better place. He is the greatest destination.

So, you who need love, look to your Husband.

You who are lost, your Savior saves gladly.

You who are dead, He is Resurrection and Life.

You who are lonely, He is the most faithful friend.

You who are sick, The Healer's hands still drip with balm.

You who doubt, the stars and the night sky are your Creator's canvas.

You who suffer, the Sufferer draws near.

To the powerless, the Baptizer burns before you.

To those in chaos, He is King.

To the wayward and independent, He is a loving Lord

To the hard of heart, the Fairest of Ten Thousand approaches you with a loving glare in His eye.

To the blind of soul, behold the crucified Lamb who stares through you with passionate love.

To the fearful, He has overcome.

There are few people alive that I enjoy talking about Jesus with more than Eric Gilmour. He is obsessed. He is my dearest friend. God has used Eric to lift my soul above the flurry so many times. The Holy Spirit has not only given Him Heavenly wording but Eric has remained with the Lamb long enough for our precious Bridegroom to permeate his tone. Eric, you are a treasure to me and my family. You are a gift to this generation and the many after us. You are a friend of the Friend of our souls and for that it's my honor to be your friend. I love and honor you.

—MICHAEL KOULIANOS, *JESUS IMAGE*

INTRODUCTION

My goal with this book is to crack the door to the King's chamber so that one light ray from the beauty of His person will blind your heart to every other desire. The Christian life is far easier than many men have made it out to be and it's far more pleasurable than many have described. There is simply no need to search for other routes. There is no reason to give attention to other things. By the giving of the Spirit, Christ has installed Himself within us. The fullness of Jesus is in the Spirit and by Him we have the fulfillment of all desires, empowerment for every work and freedom from every oppression. We are free from the need to have anything else. A.W. Tozer once wrote, *"A man who has met God is not looking for anything because He has found it."*

The longer I walk with God, the more I see that He is continually stripping me down to simplicity. The more I come to know Jesus the more I see that He has made everything so simple and easy for us. All of the difficulties that come from additions and complexities cause unnecessary frustration and discouragement. To stay simple is the true mark of genuine spirituality. Paul's only fear was that the church would be "led astray from the simplicity...of Jesus." He made a radical decision to reject any additions to "Christ and Him crucified. "

The whole of Christianity can be summed up in the symbol of the cross. It consists of both a horizontal and vertical beam. The vertical beam represents God coming down to men and men going up to God. The horizontal beam represents the work of the gospel on earth. If you take one away from the other, you're missing something and you don't have the fullness of Christianity. In fact, the horizontal beam of ministry is held up by the vertical beam of ministry unto the Lord. As important as those things are, in this book, I am not going to discuss the horizontal side of things. This book is dedicated to our ministry unto the Lord. I want to talk about *you* and *God*. I want to write this to every mom, dad, son, daughter, grandma, grandpa, husband and wife; every young person, old person and all in between. This topic of union with God exempts *no one.*

We cannot miss this topic. If we do, we miss the bullseye. Often, in conferences and settings where beautiful oration is given, miracles are breaking out, and platform ministry is manifesting at its finest, the mother who changes diapers all day can begin to feel irrelevant or less significant. Let me tell you, you can change diapers to the glory of God if your heart is set on Jesus. Most of you reading this will probably never preach a crusade, yet you have every bit as much value and importance to God as those who hold a microphone.

Success in Christianity is not seeing miracles, calling out spot-on words of knowledge or prophesying with precision. Success in Christianity is when the heart is fixed on looking to the beauty of the person of the Lord and *living* in His presence. One slight glimpse of Jesus causes all other concerns to melt away. The rays of His radiance blind us to everything else.

Let me explain to you how incredible this New Covenant is. In the scriptures, Jesus was standing physically in front of the disciples. They could reach out and touch Him. They could see Him. They could hear His voice with their own physical ears. In the midst of such an indescribable life situation, Jesus said to them, *"What you have right now is far inferior to that which is coming."* I cannot think of anything greater than seeing Jesus face to face, but Jesus could! What did He see? He saw Himself not merely dwelling *with* us but *inside* of us by the Holy Spirit.

The Holy Spirit was sent as a limitless continuation of Christ's life in the earth. Not only that, but Jesus called Him *The Comforter*. I don't know about you but I'm not interested in a comfort that I cannot *feel*. Too many in the body of Christ have slighted feelings, yet Christ referred to the Spirit of God as a *feeling*. Can you feel comfort? Absolutely.

He is a comforter who comes in and performs a work so deep in the soul that it's as if heaven is already here. This is what the Holy Ghost does. Without the Holy Spirit everything is miserable. My wife and I get to travel together and when we do we find that oftentimes the church is miserable—ministers included. There is very little joy. I don't know all the reasons why—but I know *what* and *who* the source is, for the fruit of *the Spirit* is joy (see Galatians 5).

I pray that as you read this book you will experience the reality of the Spirit's presence drawing you to fellowship with the Father in the person of Jesus Christ. May the bliss of union be an every day experience in your life. May you lay down your entire life before Jesus *the one and only*, and return to the thrill of living in the heights of *first love*.

CHAPTER ONE

JESUS IS ENOUGH

"IF WE LOVE HIM PARTIALLY, THERE WILL ALWAYS BE AN AREA THAT HE IS UNABLE TO FULFILL."

"He who comes from above is above all, he who is of the earth is from the earth and speaks of the earth. He who comes from heaven is above all." (John 3:31)

These words came from the mouth of John the Baptist. John the Baptist was the one who was filled with the Spirit and set apart for one purpose: *to clear the way for Jesus. This means, He was to remove anything and everything that would get in front of Jesus.* Notice the first phrase in the passage, "He who comes from above is above all." The word *all* does not merely mean *all people.* It means *all things* as well. He is high above anything that you could think of, any name you could name and every event that could take place. Here, John the Baptist is trying to call our attention to this one, singular superior Man, Christ Jesus.

In the eighteenth verse of the first chapter of John, the author refers to Jesus as the "one and only." Let's hit the pause button on this phrase. The *one* means, *there are no others. Only* means, *there will never be another.* He stands high above all and remains high above all. When Jesus came on the scene, John the Baptist declared, "Behold, the Lamb!" When you flip to the book of Revelation, you see that in the end we are singing, worshipping and beholding the Lamb.

So it all starts with beholding the Lamb and ends with us beholding the Lamb. There is nothing else to do but to look at the Lamb. This bothers many people. They want to stay busy with other exploits. Yet Christ said to look at Him is the only thing that is necessary. You might say, "But Eric aren't there other things to do?" No! The more you look at Him, the more you look like Him, and from there—you effortlessly do *His things*. In this, you are not making a list and checking off items, making sure you look like Jesus. No, you bypass the headache and sweat of efforts by looking to Him. Here we accomplish more by accident than we ever did on purpose.

God is more interested in His Son than anything else. It took 1600 years to put the Bible together, all to say one word: *JESUS*. He has got in His heart a sound, a melody if you will, and it is purely and only the person of Jesus. God's heart throbs and beats for Jesus. I believe many of us suffer in various areas of our lives simply because we've lost our love interest in Jesus. I believe that you could pin every personal problem back to a *deviated gaze*. At some point, somewhere along the way Jesus got replaced. "Yeah but Eric, I've never replaced Jesus." Well then, perhaps you've *added* to Him. The moment you *add* to Jesus, you've subtracted from your life. Every addition to Him is a subtraction.

We become so taken up with ourselves and so "me minded" that we lose the excitement of His name. This beautiful name was given to Him by His Father and sent to the earth by an angel. "You shall call His name Jesus" (see Matthew 1:21). It's by this wonderful name that God performs all His works. Everything that God is going to do is inside of this wonderful, beautiful, matchless, divine name above every name: *Jesus*.

There is nothing more powerful, yet there is nothing more tender. You find quickly as you walk with the Lord that this name heals the sick, breaks every oppression and cleanses the weak sinner. This name is above all. I feel in my heart that God wants to refocus, recenter and refix everything back on Jesus. Perhaps you're already walking with the revelation of Jesus. Then let this chapter be music to your soul. May God further solidify your *only*. I am writing to carve into every reader one phrase, "He who is from above is above all." May it be so deeply written on your heart that it changes your way of life, what you value and how you spend your time.

Francis de Sales once said, "We've become more occupied with love than the Beloved." I would venture to add that these days, we've become more occupied with *miracles* than the Beloved. We have a higher value for logic than His love. A lot of times, we get more occupied with *ministry* than the Beloved. A dear friend of mine got a job that he really wanted. He wanted to use his workplace as a mission field. His plan was to go into the workplace and preach Jesus. So he gets there, and they show him what he will be doing. He recognized that he would be all by himself all day long. He said, "Lord, there's no one to minister to." The Lord responded. "What about Me?" What a response! "What about Me?" How often do we allow ministry to people to eclipse our ministry to the Lord?

Perhaps your life is not going the way you thought. Maybe you thought you were going to be the next Daniel Kolenda or the next Billy Graham. Yet you find yourself at home changing diapers. You are not without One whom you can minister to. There is no higher ministry than to minister to the Lord. It's the secret to happiness and a fulfilled life. This high place is reached by going low.

We must ask Him to *take us up*. Even as you read this, begin to say to the Lord, "Take me up with You." Jesus is the uncontested pinnacle. What is a pinnacle? The highest point where only He remains. Jesus is in the heights and no one else can dwell there. If you want to come and live with Him there, you cannot bring anything with you. Many times, folks want to dwell with the Lord and enjoy the sweetness of His presence but they drag all of their stuff with them. Yet you cannot take all of your *things.* You cannot bring anything, you must receive Him as your *only thing*. That Pinnacle Place will receive nothing but *you*. So your life must be reduced to one cry: *only You Lord!*

As long as you hold onto all of these other things, He cannot be what He wants to be completely *through* and *to* you. If we love Him partially, there will always be an area that He is unable to fulfill.

> "Take me to the pinnacle above,
>
> with You my love.
>
> Where all others fall off

and my heart becomes soft.

And my mind is solved

and my will is dissolved.

Cause me to see

Continually,

 that I might always be

captivated by Your beauty.

So take me up Lord,

higher,

to be with You

above my concerns

and my plans and my needs,

my preparations, my desires, my dreams...

above callings and giftings and streams

and the thinking of all lower themes.

Take me up, Lord,

and let me see Your face shine.

Carry me to You,

and blind me too,

so that I can become new.

Where so few are lost ecstatically fastened to You

Confine me near,

align me so I can hear,

fearing no more

nor restricted by ceilings or floors.

To the depths and the heights of your person, take me Lord.

Free me

and make me believe Thee,

blissfully,

oh to be

His only!"

CHAPTER TWO

JESUS IS ENOUGH

PART TWO

"Let us have a radical commitment to be reduced to *only Jesus*."

Arthur Burt once wrote "Our *bowing* must be as our *breathing*." Our bowing is our heart cry of, "I give You my attention, I worship You, Lord. You have my heart." This must be so regular and consistent that it is as breathing. We breathe to stay alive physically and we bow to stay alive spiritually.

Here is the cure for anxiety, the victory over all sin, the healing that you've been seeking for your heart, the strength to conquer, the bloom and the blossom of all fruit: *Jesus*. The *one* and the *only*! You might think this sounds redundant. So be it. I'll be redundant forever: It's Jesus, upon Jesus, upon Jesus, upon Jesus! I call my friends sometimes and ask, "What did you preach on tonight?" The answer: "Jesus." I say, "What are you going to preach on tomorrow?" The answer stays the same: "Jesus!"

This is the beautiful redundancy of Christianity: Jesus. We have *one* message. There is only one thing to say, and one thing to offer: *Jesus!* We've got to get this on the inside, recognize it and believe it so we never stray into strange streams. Let us have a radical commitment to be reduced to *only Jesus*. I want people to be liberated by such a breed: the Jesus breed. Let us be a *Jesus people* that cannot stop proclaiming the lowly Son of God and Son of man.

The fact that Jesus is called the one and the only means that nothing else exists in the mind of God. Consider Abraham and Isaac. God says to Abraham, "Take your son...your only son." Wait a minute. Abraham already had

Ishmael at that point. Yet God refers to Isaac as, "Abraham's only son." Why? Because to God, the only thing that existed was the *son of promise*. So it is with much of what is going on in the church today. We cry this or that Christian themed thing and God says, "I have one Son. One thought. One desire. One happiness. One goal. One purpose. My Son."

If it's not in Him, to Him and through Him, it doesn't exist in the eyes of God. That means your ministry exploits, ventures and all. One will say, "Yeah, but Eric we have all sorts of fruit popping up." Forget your fruit, *He is the fruit.* The only test is, *did it come from Him and go back to Him?* It's the only litmus test we have. He is the answer to all things. "Come to me," was not a mere religious idea, but the very prescription mankind needed for all of life. The "One Thing" is the only necessity for life.

> Christ's wisdom is Himself.
>
> His answer is Himself.
>
> He is Adam's only hope,
>
> Enoch's kidnapper,
>
> the face that Moses longed to see.
>
> Paul's only fear was that they would go into something more than Jesus.

Paul's only determination was to know no addition to Jesus.

James' caution was to love nothing but Him.

Peter's advice was to look at Jesus like a lamp shining in a dark place. What an image! If you're in a room that has no light, then suddenly you light a match, you can see that light and nothing else. In other words, pay attention to Jesus as if He is the only visible thing in the room. C.S. Lewis said, "Not only do I see You, but *by You, I see.*" Pay attention to Christ like a lamp shining in a dark place.

In the scriptures, David was pining for something. What else could He be pining for? What does *pining* mean? To have a soul that suffers out of desire for Him. David suffered on the inside longing for *somebody*. It was God whom he longed for.

Isaiah had a blessing he released when he said, "How blessed are those that long for Him."

Solomon painted a picture in his allegorical story of Song of Solomon when he cried out in lovesickness, "Let Him hold you...never let Him go."

Hosea cried out, "Marry me!" Many of the other prophets cried out things like, "Injustice!" Hosea was different. He said, "You've forgotten Him."

The last time God ever gave a command with His mouth in

the earth was when He said, "This is My Son. Listen to Him." He never revoked this command. He gave it, and it still lives today like the day that He gave it. *Listen to Jesus. Give Him all of your attention.* That's where it ended with God.

Mary cherished Him in her heart. Mary of Bethany saw His presence as more important than answers. Her brother was dead, yet she threw herself at His feet. His presence was more important than people, answers and explanations. She reserved nothing from Him.

Abraham shows us that God was more precious than His promises. You might think, Abraham's dealings were with the Father God. Yet Christ said, "Before Abraham was, I AM."

Jacob cried out something strange, "Touch me!"

Perhaps you're like some of these patriarchs. Maybe you've experienced the heart cry of Jacob for the touch of the Lord. God loves this the most, when His people pine for Him.

He seeks to be sought, He longs to be longed for, He waits to be wanted!

He is all yours, given completely. For He is the fullness of grace and truth. Jesus is the greatest message from start to finish. We endure by seeing Him.

Maturity in the Christian life is maintaining a radical reduction to Jesus and only Jesus. The Spirit enables us to see Jesus, and it is in Jesus that we are enabled to see God. God put His fullness in the Son of Man to meet with man in the earth.

God has reserved His face for the Son. This is why Moses' cry to see His face was denied. Jesus the face of God was reserved for the specific time when God would break the heavens open and descend into the womb of a virgin.

> He is greater than the angels, higher than the priests,
>
> Every knee will bow to His exalted seat.
>
> Seven stars in His hand, every crown is at His feet.
>
> Complete and perfect are His ways, He is the ancient of days!
>
> The earth and sky flee from His face,
>
> He is a person, a taste, a resting place—a refuge in any case.
>
> Oh, for the day when our faith shall be sight,
>
> And because He is bright the bride's clothes turn to white.
>
> He's the lamp in the night,
>
> And the end to all fights.
>
> He is all power and might,
>
> He is light, life, and love—Jesus above!

What is the message? To look at the Lamb and to call everyone else to do the same. This is the model of John the Baptist. He beheld the Lamb and proceeded to say, "Behold, the Lamb!" Jesus seeks a single-eyed bride.

SEEING JESUS

> "Behold the Lamb of God…" (John 1:29)

We look to Him and live. I once read a tweet that said, "the essential Christian message is not *behave,* but *BEHOLD!*"

> We live by looking.
>
> When I stop looking at Him,
>
> I stop seeing Him.
>
> When I stop seeing Him,
>
> I stop desiring Him.
>
> When I stop desiring Him,
>
> I start looking for *other things.*

John Piper said, "Sin is what you do when you're not satisfied with God."

Holiness is the fruit of being addicted to the maximum pleasure of life, which is God Himself. Are you dealing with sin? Look at the Lamb.

Are you struggling with deep rooted issues?

Look at the Lamb.

There's nothing too deep for Him. Only looking at the Lamb can plunge deep enough to get to the root of your person. You can check yourself into programs, learn meditative practices and pursue odd guru-oriented stuff. Even the Christian guru stuff won't work if we aren't looking at the Lamb. The only wise counsel someone can give is to direct you to the Wonderful Counselor.

Often, we go on and on, plugging ourselves into various movements. All the while, Jesus is forgotten. He is put on the shelf. Regarded as a mere *good man* while we pursue other things. Yet, until we have Him, we have nothing. It is Jesus, and only Jesus. You cannot even *want Him* without Him. You cannot *love Him,* without Him. You cannot even *recognize Him*, without Him.

Once you believe this, you will never live another day without throwing yourself at His feet declaring, "You must be *all* to me today." We go to the Lord to receive desire for the Lord. Everytime I throw myself at His feet, He quickens me to life and love with the vision of His person, then and only then can I love Him! I find myself saying, "Lord, help me love you the way you deserve to be loved. Help me give you the attention you deserve."

I remember Michael Koulianos said to me, "In order for my heart to love Him constantly, my eyes must see Him constantly." When he said that to me, it hit me like a ton of bricks. It's the secret: looking unto Jesus. He is the author (He begins it) and the finisher (the One who brings it all the way to completion). Leonard Ravenhill was asked at the end of his life, "How did you stay so faithful to God after all these years?" He answered, "By looking unto Jesus."

Beholding Jesus is not a means. What do I mean by *a means*? Jesus is not a way of getting stuff. When you say, "I'm going to look to Jesus so that I can [fill in the blank]," you're adding to Him. Forget the answer you need. He is the answer you need. Some say, "I need to work on my joy." Forget your joy! Look to Jesus. It's in Him that all consists. Don't seek after peace, patience and self control. Look at Jesus He will be all of those other things.

When you shift away from Jesus, one of the first symptoms that ensues is that you get weary. Jesus says, "If you come to Me, I'll give you rest." So a life of rest is a life that perpetually comes to Jesus. What we do in the time of victory is the same thing we do in the time of failure, we must *come to Jesus*. His feet are our pillow. His feet are our crown. Laying and looking at His feet is how we attain eyes to see the world the way He has called us to. Many become weary by departing from this place of rest, and the way they see the world is eschew, even if their language is right. The danger of the intimacy movement is that many people have merely adopted the language.

JESUS IS ENOUGH | 19

In Christianity, we've often adopted a Christian vocabulary rather than a Christ-experience. We slip into these things, yet the remedy is very easy: *look*. Just recognize that you haven't been looking and turn to look at Him. He made it simple. There are many results when you look at Jesus. Yet once you see Him, you forget them all. They just start happening. Things begin to take shape without your effort.

> As was said to an old saint when visited by the Lord...
>
> Do you desire good things?
>
> There is none good but Me.
>
> Do you desire blessing?
>
> Who is more blessed than Me?
>
> Do you desire power?
>
> Who is more powerful than Me?
>
> Do you desire spiritual heights?
>
> Am I not the pinnacle?
>
> Do you desire riches?
>
> Are they not hidden in Me?.
>
> Do you desire wisdom?
>
> Who is more wise than Me?
>
> Do you desire help?

> Who can help you but Me?
>
> Do you seek peace?
>
> Am I not the Prince of Peace?
>
> Do you seek life?
>
> Am I not life itself?
>
> Do you desire beauty?
>
> Who is more beautiful than Me?

I ask you: what is more attractive to you than spending time with Jesus? Answering this question is how you discover that which stands between you and God. What gets more of your attention than Jesus? What moves your heart more than Jesus? In that answer, you discover the reason why experiencing the bliss of His presence is not a daily reality for you.

See, when you choose to marry Him, you've let go of everything to *just* have Him. When you choose to marry Him, you have chosen to let go of everything else and only have *Him*. "Forsaking all others, keeping only to You." *This* is the beauty of the New Covenant. This is the wonder of marriage to Christ. We now look to Him to be peace. Not our spouses. We look to Him to be joy. Not circumstances going our way. We look to Him for fulfillment. Not gaining all the things that we want.

Because of the greatness of His majesty, to proclaim

anything else is the greatest tragedy. Sometimes we forget how beautiful He is. Every time I see Him, I ask Him to forgive me for forgetting how beautiful He is. There is a human propensity to leave dependency. Without loving Him, we never find satisfaction. I remember Michael Koulianos gave me a Bible once and he wrote on the inside, "Love Him. That's enough."

Even prayer can turn into friction if it's without the tender love for Him in our soul. Sometimes we put prayer in His place. Many people stray into high spiritual exercises and routines of disciplines and responsibilities and all the while forget the living Lover of their souls. Do you know what the product of that equation is? *Pride*. I hear people say boastfully, "Man, I fasted for 40 days." Firstly, why are you telling me? Secondly, does that make you great or something? As humans, we love this stuff. We are attracted to having a wonderful, high appearance. Heidi Baker said, "How can I stand on a platform and pretend to be something when He became nothing?"

Most, if not *all* of our internal issues would be solved and dissolved by just clinging to Him a little bit more seriously in our lives. Many of us want to be instantaneously delivered from everything that oppresses us and bothers us so that we don't actually have to cling to Jesus. A.B. Simpson said, "I have found the spiritual secret: it is drawing Christ…breath by breath." There it is! A perpetual, "I need you."

CHAPTER THREE

JESUS OUR KING

"Just as water seeks to fill the lowest place, the Holy Spirit will rush in to fill those that are low."

"Behold, thy King cometh, meek…" (Matthew 21:5 KJV)

Take note, the passage above did not say, "Behold, thy King cometh, powerful…" nor did it say, "Behold, thy King cometh, wise…" Is He wise? Of course. He *is* wisdom. Is He powerful? Absolutely. More than any other. Yet the passage emphasizes a very *specific* way that He comes: *in meekness*. For meekness marks the *arrival* of Jesus.

> "Come to Me, all who are weary and heavy-laden, and I will give you rest. Take My yoke upon you and learn from Me, for I am gentle and humble…" (Matthew 11:28-29)

The one time that Jesus opens His mouth to describe His own character, He chooses this word: *humble*. If there is one thing that Jesus wants you to understand about what and who He is, He chooses the word humble. He could have chosen any other word to describe Himself yet He chose *humble*. See, He knew you and me, and that in the midst of His greatness, majesty and splendor, we would likely try to separate Him from His core internal reality which is *humility*.

Men are attracted to all kinds of God's *externals*. Yet when they are presented with God's *internals* they often lose interest. Yet this is very attribute is what *houses* the presence of God. Jesus was the tabernacle of God, was He not? He was the home of God in the earth—the living, walking, manifestation of God's infinite glory. And He essentially says, *if you're going to be a carrier of the glory, this is the characteristic that must be yours: humility.* If you learn anything about me, learn this, "I am humble." We would rather hear Him say, "The carriers of the glory are disciplined and strong." However, humility is the character of Christ. One may see Jesus as this or that, yet He forever settles His character as humility.

If "He also predestined [us] to become conformed to the image of His Son" (Romans 8:29). God wants us to look just like Jesus. If the Spirit works into us the nature of Jesus, then this is what submission to Him will produce. Jesus is humble. May *His* be *ours*. The New Covenant scriptures go on to say, "But He gives a greater grace. Therefore it says, 'God is opposed to the proud, but gives grace to the humble.'" (James 4:6).

Like a fountain from heaven, grace is continually, perpetually poured into those who are humble. The opposite is true to those who lack humility: God resists them. In other words, He prohibits their entrance into His presence. In fact, the word *opposes* in the passage means to put your foot down to block the door from being opened. God literally blocks entrance to those who are full of pride. What is pride? Anything and everything that is not humble.

Pride is resisted by God.

Pride drains grace,

blinds us to His face,

withers men into snakes.

It is flight from God's help,

the custodian of hell,

the fortress of lusts,

it threw angels to dust,

it's the devil's cusp,

Lucifer's invention and God's only prevention.

We must hate it. Because we cannot fight Satan with Satan. Andrew Murray said, "Jesus came to bring humility back into the earth." Look at the pattern we see in the Old Testament that coincides with this statement:

> "For the Lord of hosts will have a day of reckoning against everyone who is proud and lofty." (Isaiah 2:12)

> "The pride of man will be humbled." (Isaiah 2:17)

> "Everyone who is proud in heart is an abomination to the Lord." (Proverbs 16:5)

> "But when his heart was lifted up and his spirit became so proud that he behaved arrogantly, he was deposed from his royal throne and his glory was taken away from him." (Daniel 5:20)

You see similar passages throughout the Old Testament, where the prophets saw that God was going to make something right in the earth. What was that something? To bring low the proud. The problem He sees with the earth is that we are proud. This is God's issue with humanity, that we think we are *something* apart from Him. I feel that the Lord is saying, "Pride provokes me." Pride makes man His enemy. Nothing is so opposed to God as the self sufficiency of *pride*.

Pride is selfishness, self-glory, self-effort, self-exaltation and self-consciousness. It's all about me, me, me and more me. Vance Havner said, "If God came to save us, He came to save us from *I, myself and me. If He didn't come to save us from self infatuation, I don't know what the Savior came to do.*" The greatest hindrance to everything that God wants to do in your life is *your eyes fixed on you*. Keith Green sung it well, "It's so hard to see when my eyes are on me."

> "The fear of the Lord is to hate evil; pride and arrogance and the evil way." (Proverbs 8:13)

James remedies this by saying, "Humble yourselves in the presence of the Lord..." (James 4:10.) We see the scriptures again link together two things: *humility* and *the presence of the Lord*. They are connected, for God sews them together.

Did you know, there is a difference between *humility* and actually *humbling yourself*? *Humility* is Jesus' character. *Humbling yourself* is bringing everything low to His feet. It's like this: when you humble yourself the Lord will exalt you. Humbling yourself means bringing everything down to the feet of Jesus then from that place God exalts you into the humility of Christ.

When He exalts you, He doesn't bring you *out* of humility. In fact, when He exalts you, He brings you up into the heights and glory of what true humility actually is. Humility is the character and nature of Christ. Humbling yourself is bowing low in honest bankruptcy before God where you're able to lay in front of Him your very heart, motives, intentions, expectations, desires, your own family, possessions, your calling, gifts, past, present and future.

If Jesus sat physically in front of you right now and said, "We've got to have a meeting about your heart," then the moment you made eye contact with Him, you would immediately see all of the things in your heart that oppose Him. You would become overwhelmingly aware of everything that is not as pure as He is; impure motives, how you responded the a situation the other day, sin that's been hidden for a long time and more. Yet He would look at you with love. And if you had any sense at all you would look back at Him and say, "Here. Have it all. I'm broken, weak, and empty. I'm in dire need of You, Lord. Take my heart and my whole life."

If we go low before the Lord, He will rush in and fill us. Just as water seeks to fill the lowest place, the Holy Spirit will rush in to fill those that are low. Those that are low will be filled with God's presence. This why so many are dry, because they are *too high*. When you go low, you find the riches of God's presence.

The reason why God raises up those who are bowed down is that those who are bowed down have renounced any desire to be raised up at all. They left it all at His feet.

This is our Christ whose humility is dually shown, in what He put off (heaven) and what He put on (humanity): lowly, meek and humble. He could have *always* taught standing on the water. He chose not to, because He is humble.

> "I am among you as the one who serves." (Luke 22:27)

Did you hear what Jesus said here? God who created all things and sustains all things by the power of His own words literally says, "I have come to you *to serve you*." What is a servant? One who puts the needs of another above his own. There's nothing like this in the universe. This is God's disposition. See, people ask me, "How can I tell if I have the same servant-heart that Jesus had?" I'll tell you one good way: *how do you react when someone treats you like a servant?*

This will be a good measuring stick to determine where our heart is. When someone else is exalted above you, how do you react? If your desire is to lift up everyone above yourself then you can only rejoice for those who are lifted up, because your goal is being accomplished! You will only feel competition and comparison to the degree that you've placed yourself higher than others. We must throw ourselves down at the feet of Jesus for in humbling ourselves, we will find the riches of His character producing presence.

CHAPTER FOUR

HOW TO EXPERIENCE JESUS AS ENOUGH

"THE *HOLIEST* OF ALL WAS THE *HUMBLEST* OF ALL."

"But the greatest among you shall be your servant. Whoever exalts himself shall be humbled; and whoever humbles himself shall be exalted." (Matthew 23:11-12)

Let me tell you what Christ is *not* saying here: if you choose to go to that humble place, I'll come and rescue you out of that humility. If you choose to serve others, I'll come and make it so that one day you'll be served. No, that's *not* what He is saying. He is saying, *when you really understand who I am you'll see that the highest place is the lowest place.* Serving others is not *how you get* to the highest place. It *is* the highest place.

This is how you walk in His presence. Everything contrary to humility cannot house the presence of God. As many of you reading this know, I host events called *The School of His Presence* all over the world. I share at length on enjoying God's presence, communion with the Lord and the blissful joy of walking with Jesus. I'd love to share on these things all the time. Yet I find people everywhere who say, "I don't have that kind of life. I stumble upon God here or there but I don't daily enjoy Him." I'll tell you the number one reason why: they are too high. They are looking for the great "somethings" when Christ is found in being nothing.

God only stays in humble residences. You want to abide in Him and to have Him abide in you? It will take place in low places. I'm amazed at how little humility is talked about. Especially considering that it is the root of child-likeness. Childlikeness is the absence of self-consciousness. When you get that, you find the key to the Kingdom of Heaven. The humble childlike loss of self. What is the kingdom of heaven? All the riches there are in Jesus Christ. All the wonders of His person are accessed through child-likeness, for the kingdom is given freely to the children. Yet when you're self-conscious, you are no longer child-like. There is too much pride to abide. *Bride* and *pride* will never mix.

Humility is the one indispensable condition for fellowship with God. To God, the lowly heart is the chief mark of following the lovely Lamb of God. In my earlier days I would seek God and wanted to levitate or glow or have some type of distinguishing sign and wonder that set me apart from everyone else. I would pray, "Lord make me a glowing saint." I wanted demons to manifest at the sound of my voice. I wanted to heal people with my shadow. This was my goal. Lofty, to say the least. Yet now, it is so different. My life giving glimpses of Jesus and His love have broken me down. I find my prayers are now, "Make me a servant, humble and true. Make me meek Lord, and lowly like You." For I see that *here* is where God dwells.

Last year, my wife asked me, "If you could have absolutely anything for your birthday what would it be?" I allowed my mind to limitlessly dream of the possibility of having anything I could ever ask for. As one thing rose after another, I felt a desire for humility rise up in my heart. Then with tears in my eyes I said, "How much is a humble heart?" No one can give you humility but Jesus. No one can humble you, for you. You've got to *choose* to humble yourself. I cannot be humble for you, and you cannot be humble for me.

See, Satan breathed pride into Adam and he sprang forth a humanity that had no room for God. Daniel Kolenda once told me, "God will send no one home empty except those that are full of themselves." Andrew Murray said, "Without humbling ourselves there can be no true abiding in God's presence or experiencing His favor."

Humility is the key fruit of the presence of God. The *holiest* of all was the *humblest* of all. We must have a fresh desire to be humble. Humility puts me where I am supposed to be and puts God where He is supposed to be. Humbling yourself alone allows God to do everything for you. You are still in control to the degree that you don't humble yourself. To the degree you don't humble yourself, you are still operating on a battery pack that's really low. Yet God is always maxed out, and limited by nothing.

Murray said, "Humility is the displacement of self and the enthronement of God." Do you want God to rule your life? Humbling yourself at His feet is how He does this. Jesus is humility personified. We see Him manifest this through a statement in the gospels, "Truly, truly, I say to you, the Son can do nothing of Himself…" (John 5:19). True humility is a declaration that you can do *nothing* on your own. Later in the chapter, Christ continues with similar sentiments, "I can do nothing on

My own initiative" (John 5:30). With these passages, not only is He confessing His inability do anything on His own but also stating that He refuses to *try* to do anything on His own.

> "So Jesus answered them and said, 'My teaching is not Mine, but His who sent Me.'" (John 7:16)

> "So Jesus said, 'When you lift up the Son of Man, then you will know that I am He, and I do nothing on My own initiative.'" (John 8:28)

> "But I do not seek My glory." (John 8:50)

Jesus teaches complete bankruptcy before God. Jesus teaches us that the true spiritual life is one of absolute self-renunciation. All of these maxims on humility that Christ uttered were to draw us to a simple reality that *this* is how we walk with God. Yet so often we get in the way and make it far more difficult than it should be.

People have said to me, "The Christian life is so hard." No, it's not. If it is difficult, the yoke that you are wearing is not His. You are wearing your own yoke. His yoke is easy and His burden is light. The yoke you have is one of sin and pride. This is why men are so restless and itching to make themselves something. They attempt to increase in power or seek gain, and gifts. Men are frenzied scattered in a million directions. This is why they cannot get along with their brothers. Prideful people are always looking down on others...and if you're looking down, you cannot see Him who is above all.

We must keep our hearts before God if we are going to walk in His presence. Many times we are reluctant to give everything to God because we feel like we will lose something, or lose control. One of the major issues in our lives, and I include my life in this: *control*. Some say, "I fear to give this to you, Lord. I don't know what you'll do with it." I want to tell you, nothing is safe that is not committed to Him.

We fear to commit our life to Him out of fear for the safety of it, yet I'm telling you, unless it is committed to Him, it is in danger. Your very own life, your very own family are all in danger if not given to the Lord. He alone can protect us. Yet if man relinquishes all to God then God can be all through man. If we give it all into His hands then our lives rest safe in the hands of God. God is unable to pass through whatever you do not relinquish. He is unable to fulfill whatever is kept from Him. This is why we have people who are completely developed in one area but totally lopsided in another. It is *total surrender* that creates a balanced life.

Humility is literally Christ's presence through your character. Many people see wonderful, delightful things in the scriptures such as peace that surpasses all understanding, joy unspeakable, the fellowship of bliss with the Savior. They see these things in the text but they feel as though they are unable to actually apprehend them. Maybe you've read the text that says, "He whom the Son sets free is free indeed," and you've said, "That's wonderful. I believe it. But how come it isn't free for me?"

There once was a little boy outside of the candy shop. As he was peering through the window and admiring all of the candies the owner of the shop said to the boy, "Hey son, do you like candy?" The boy responds, "Yeah!" The owner says, "Take whatever you want!" The boy says, "I can't!" The owner says, "Why not?" The boy says, "Because there is a thick plate of glass between me and all the candy!"

This illustrates the point, that thick plate of glass between you and all of the promises of God is pride. You can see all He has. You can admire it. But every time you reach out, there is a hindrance keeping you from tasting and experiencing the joy, peace and fulfillment that God has for you. There's a lot that God wants to give you. But first He must have you. Let Him *take you*; then and only then can He *give Himself to you.*

CHAPTER FIVE

HOW TO EXPERIENCE JESUS AS ENOUGH

PART TWO

"God will smile on one humble man over a million gifted men."

ONLY IF HE IS *EVERYTHING* CAN HE SAFELY GIVE US *ANYTHING*. One of my favorite quotes of all time is from Andrew Murray in which he said, "The insignificances of daily life are the tests of eternity because they prove what spirit really possesses us." You might think, "There are a lot of big words there, Eric. What do you mean?" I'm saying this: your humility will be seen in the common course of your life. The way you hear and respond to other folks in your day to day walk will be a manifestation of that which already resides on the inside of you. In these common settings you will see if humility is real. Humility is not seen on stage. It's not in what someone says of themselves. Humility is seen in the most unguarded moments of life. You know who will see that first? Your wife. Your husband. Leonard Ravenhill said, "Don't tell me how godly you are. Let me talk to your wife."

I want to be possessed by God. I want the real thing. I don't want this in order to merely stand before a crowd and read their mail, rip casts off of folks, and perform signs and wonders. I want *humility*. I don't want to stand and do those things if my heart is distant from being a residence for God's presence. You can go to hell with gifts. Praise God for gifts and we ought to pursue them but the reality is this: if you don't look like Jesus on the inside, you are not going into the kingdom with Him.

The soul that can truly say, "I have lost myself in finding you," is the soul that no longer compares itself with other people. Why? Because they are no longer in the equation.

It is said, "Comparison is the thief of joy." Some people are miserable because they are constantly comparing what they have and don't have compared to those around them. If this describes you, then it is safe to say that you have not lost yourself in finding Him. But if you do, you'll recognize that comparing yourself with other people only means you've failed to find all you need in God.

You might wonder, *what does all of this have to do with Jesus being enough?* The answer: *everything.* It is a matter of Him *coming in,* instead of Him *giving us what we need.*

I was once praying for people in a prayer line. When I got to one girl, I put my hand on her head and I had a vision. In the vision I saw that Jesus was trying to get her to put her head on His chest. She was stiff-necked and refused to yield to His gentle desire to hold her. See, when we lay our head on His breast, we gain access to the divine treasure chest. She was blocking this intimate rest. Do you know what this is called? Stubbornness. Stubborn means, *a resolute adherence to your own will.* That is pride and it will kill you.

True humility not only gives itself completely over to being only His, but it looks upon the most feeble person in the room and treats them as if they are the son of a king. C.S. Lewis said, "A humble person doesn't go around telling you how terrible he is. A humble person will simply have a true interest in the things coming out of your mouth." We are so prideful that while other people are talking, all we are thinking about is our own lives or our own rebuttal and response. We have a hard time looking at someone directly in the eyes and giving them full attention. Do you know why? Because our lives are all about us. A key to the glory of God being walked out in your life is to be humble enough to listen and receive from everyone around you.

Many of us cannot bear someone being better treated than us or praised over us. It is because we are the center of our own attention. We crave to be special. We crave applause and admiration. You'll never get back the time you waste trying to be noticed. It's worthless. But to humble ourselves at the feet of Jesus we will find that His presence will free us from the need to have anything else. We find that we don't need relevance or significance in the eyes of men. We are not craving to be a VIP or a distinguishable ministry or recognized as the "spiritual one" because in having Him we have no *need* for man to fulfill.

Even in the midst of the most spiritual environments, men can erect a monument to themselves by telling testimonies of what they have done and seen. This kind of thing makes God really upset. It provokes Him. He will not share His glory with another. God wants to purge us of these things by giving us Himself as all we could ever look for. To grant to us Himself as the end of all pursuits. When we try to erect a testimony monument of relevance in the minds of others we are acting out of a lack of satisfaction with God.

God will smile on one humble man over a million gifted

men. Did you know that Jonathan was not selfishly wanting the crown? He was selflessly concerned with it being on the right head. Praise God for such humility, for now we have the King of Kings who came through the lineage of David. If humility is not the foundation, it will all come tumbling down. Humility is the image of God in man. Pride is anti-God in every way. Yet, nothing keeps a man outside of the reach of the devil like humility.

The prideful man can be spotted by his harshness, impatience, longing to control everything, irritations, judgments, comparisons, competitions, jealousy and bitterness. All of these things are the fruit of pride. Pride has a *tone* to it. Pride speaks a certain way. Pride lifts itself above other people. Pride, above all, is the neglect of God. And the worst kind is when it is done in the name of God. Pride is sourced in its own strength.

The number one way you can spot pride in your life is when you lose the deep sense of needing Jesus moment by moment. Ingratitude sets in. If you think to yourself, *spending time with Jesus is not necessary,* then you are by definition, arrogant. If you think you can bypass Christ in this thing called living, you've lost your sense of need for Him. Humility sees every lull throughout the day is an invitation to come away and every breath as gratitude.

I received a letter one time in which a lady told me, "I've got four kids. I'm so busy. I work. There's no way I could spend time with God for 45 minutes every day." She basically rebuked me for telling people to spend time with God. She even incorporated scriptures and quotes from saints of old. It was a compelling little booklet and I almost started to agree with her case. She provided in-depth rationale for not being able to spend time with the Lord. Then it dawned on me: she probably spent three hours putting the letter together. She had three hours to rebuke me but not 45 minutes for Jesus. There's something wrong. Pride is deceptive blindness to your true state.

I told Daniel Kolenda about this woman one day, and he said to me, "If I went to her and said "I will give you two million dollars if you spend an hour with God everyday," do you think she would do it?" Absolutely. Why? Because she values the two million dollars. You can tell if you value God by whether or not you make time to be with Him. The money, for many, would have been more valuable than the presence of God. I'm not trying to slight anyone. I just want to bring us to lay our hearts open before Jesus so He can come in with tenderness and sweetness and grant us a character like unto His.

There is no pride so dangerous, so subtle, so insidious as *spiritual* pride. It slips in unconsciously and creeps in undetected. This is pride that feels satisfied with its own attainments. It's a pride that is OK with not giving itself completely to Jesus because it has everything that it wants outside of Him. What does that look like? You're finished ministering to someone, and you are on a high about what God used you to do. You feel like you just did your service for the Lord and you feel you have pleased Him and you feel less of a need to be dependent upon Him. At that point, God is no longer the source of life but a manager. God does not want to be your boss. He wants to be your bread.

When my kids fight and insist upon their own way, I say to them, "Hey, which one of you wants to be favored by God?" They stop and say, "Me, me, me!" In that, they are both wanting to give up their wills. But prior to that, they were trying to insist on their own way. I remember being in the grocery store one time and they both wanted to hold my phone. My older girl ripped the phone from my younger daughter and they began to fight over the phone. I stopped them and asked what was going on and my oldest said, "She took the phone from me and I want it!" The youngest cried out, "But I want the phone." There were two wills, both at odds.

I grabbed my oldest daughter and whispered with all the love I could, "Baby, they spit in Jesus' face." She looked at me and said, "What does that have to do with anything right now?" I said, "Honey, they spit on His face and He gave Himself up for them." She said, "Yeah but that is Jesus. He is perfect. I'm not." I said, "That's just it. He will be perfect through your humanity as He was living among humanity if you will yield to the Holy Spirit." He can be Himself through those who humble themselves through surrender to Him.

I was trying to show her that if you will yield to God in the midst of pain and not having your own way, the Holy Ghost will come in and Christ will shine through your face. You might say, "Yeah, but what if God doesn't resurrect me?" Trust me, He never fails. If you go low, He will raise you and fill you as sure as Jesus was raised from the dead. You don't ever have to worry about whether or not God will resurrect you if you die to self.

Andrew Murray prayed, "Let us flee to Jesus and hide ourselves in Him, that we may be clothed with humility."

> A twisted crown of thorns too small in size
>
> was pressed into His brow and blood flowed in His eyes
>
> blinding Him to all but the prize.
>
> This is humility personified,
>
> His back gashed opened deep and wide
>
> with whips made of sin and pride,
>
> though men love things that are deified
>
> not things that are crucified
>
> but that's God…He comes and He dies.

This is the ultimate demonstration of humility. God is calling us to freshly come to the foot of the cross. He invites us to go down low, to be raised up in newness of life and walk with the power of His grace in our lives, every single day.

> "Oh precious blood of You who loved me so,
>
> Your hands are nailed and Your head hangs low.
>
> Your body is broken, Your back is lashed open.
>
> The splintering cross is soaked in blood,
>
> Oh what love, a love of me
>
> And I see thy glory, when thy feet are upon the sea
>
> But never such glory
>
> as when they are fastened to the tree.
>
> The breath of life breathes out His ghost,
>
> a dismayed angelic host,
>
> A naked God bleeds upon a post
>
> He is mostly red,
>
> "come down," they said,
>
> men's faith is dead
>
> but *God bled*."

CHAPTER SIX

JESUS IS OUR ONE NECESSITY

"Let our love be *only* for Him and not Him *and* all of the *additions*."

"ONE THING I HAVE ASKED FROM THE LORD, THAT I SHALL seek: that I may dwell in the house of the Lord all the days of my life, to behold the beauty of the Lord. And to meditate in His temple." (Psalm 27:4)

Do you see what David is saying here? He is saying that his *one singular desire* is looking at God. The definition of prayer is *sustaining the sweet sense of His person.* That's it. It's lingering, attentiveness to Him. It's far more important that He have all of your attention, than that you know what to do. We often want to *know what to do* when what He wants is *you!* He wants your heart, affection and attention.

Throughout the Bible, the only person that ever used the phrase *one thing* like this, is David. I find it interesting that the only person that God ever asked, "What is the *one thing* that you want?" was David's son, Solomon. It was almost as if the Lord was saying to Solomon, "Could your heart be anything like your father's?"

After David had passed, God had no one crying out *one thing.* So God approaches David's offspring in pursuit of such a heart and Solomon asks for wisdom. Wisdom is a good thing and it pleased the Lord yet it still was not the *highest* thing. Why? Because it didn't keep Solomon until the end. In fact, the Bible says, "Solomon loved the Lord, but…" Often we love the Lord, yet there is a *but* on the end of our sentence. Or we say, "I love you Lord, and…" Did you catch that? It's the *ands* and *buts* added to our love that kill us. The additions are deadly. They are literally toxic. If the Christian walk is getting difficult, it's because we've added things to the equation that were never intended by God.

As wonderful as church atmospheres are, there is potential for us to latch on to so many other things. Yet there is power in our willingness to get simple. As you do this you will begin to take flight by the Spirit and you'll see that *everything* in the Spirit is easy. There's no longer a struggling to *make it through*. You're snuggling with Him instead. Your struggling is in exact proportion to your lack of snuggling.

Whenever my attention is elsewhere, I feel it in my heart. When my focus is astray I start to wander away. I always remind myself, "Without my heart laid at Your feet, it always tries to take Your seat." When you begin to compare yourself you have removed your eyes from Jesus. You have to take your eyes off of Him to put them on other things, simply put. He wants a *one thing* people. The simplicity of Jesus can cure us of the complexities of charismatic culture. Praise God for an appetite for spiritual things, but they all must come secondary to the person of Jesus. Many of you reading this are like an eagle on the ground. You've woken up, shaken off sleep, straightened out your feathers —but you haven't begun to ascend into the altitude you're called to dwell in. I encourage you to fly up above in the place that only one exists: Jesus. It's higher than gifts. It's higher than anointing. It's higher than prayers. It's bridal union with the person of Jesus! It is the experience of His kiss. His kiss will kill competition, condemnation and complexities; it's the kiss that sets your soul free. He plants kisses on your soul like seeds, the bloom and blossom of which is the fruit of the Spirit.

When your heart enters into fellowship with Jesus you begin to say things like, "You are here. What more could I want?" See, if Christianity could be likened to a pyramid, the lower you go—the more there is. The higher you go, you're only His.

His face is available for you in unlimited measure. He is inexhaustible as a person. You cannot reach the bottom. As you continually plunge the depths of Him you find that you didn't even scratch the surface yet. His greatness is unsearchable. And so now life becomes a quest to exhaust the inexhaustible riches of Jesus. I'm finding over and over again that for some reason in the midst of Christianity, so often there is something else that gets attention when there is a limitless, inexhaustible Christ. *Oh Lord, forgive us for giving the attention that You deserve to things far inferior to You.*

I want to lift Jesus high, as He is the only way to altitude, in fact, *He is the altitude.* So often, we get so heavy, burdened and bogged down with *stuff*. It's easy to look in God's direction and not look at God. We can get mesmerized with His *things* and forget *Him*. For example, I could be looking in my wife's direction, be listening to her, yet not have eye to eye contact with her. I remember looking at my wife in the kitchen one day and I was wanting her attention. She was doing motherly things. I grabbed her and said, "Give me your attention." She said, "I've got all of these things to do." I took her and grabbed her by the chin and looked her in the eyes and said, "I love you." A couple nights later I was woken up in the middle of the night by someone grabbing my chin yet there was nobody there…it was Jesus. He grabbed my chin because He wanted to lift my chin up to look directly at Him. Often our head is down, and He lifts our head, because we cannot see Him when our head is down.

Oh friend, you are the apple of God's eye. If you could see how much joy you bring to His heart you wouldn't even believe it. To believe this and remind yourself of this is very, very important. One of my favorite Christian writers said, "Prayer is looking at God and God looking at me." Tozer said, "When the eyes of the soul looking out meet the eyes of God looking in…right there, heaven has begun upon the earth." Often, God gives us things and we let them take the place of the One who gave them. As I've said before, you can cheat on God with the stuff God gave you.

Let me tell you something about God, He is jealous for you. He will not share you *nor your attention* with anything else. In fact, sometimes He hides the future from you on purpose. Why? He wants to make sure that He has all your attention. He wants you to be caught up with Him, not where you're going or even the purposes He has for you. He won't share your attention with your future. He would rather end all His purposes through you than to lose your heart's affection. You might have prayed over and over, "Lord, show me what's to come. Show me where I'm going," your desire for guidance has supplanted your desire for Him. Sometimes He blocks your view of all these things you need, to give you the only true thing you need: *Him*. He is more interested in feeding you than leading you.

Do you remember when Abraham was looking for a bride for his son? He sent his servant to find a bride for his son. The servant found the woman and when he saw her, he began to give her gifts from the bridegroom. Yes, he gave her gifts, but his ultimate intention and purpose was to take her to the bridegroom. This is *exactly* what the Spirit of God is doing now. He comes and gives gifts to point you to the Bridegroom. He wants to grab you and take you to the Bridegroom Himself! He wants to meet with you, marry you and numb you to doubt, unbelief, fear and all of the things that scatter your soul. It is a sad fact to note that many people have received the gifts and said, "Thank you for these gifts" and all the while have no intention to go on to the Bridegroom. Literally the gold in their hands has outshined the one who sent it as an indication of His beauty. We must face this question, "Will you go with this man?"

To be thrilled by Him is everything. How could we love another, when He has taken our hearts from us? When I feel temptation at times in my life, I'll say that to the Lord,

"How can I give my heart to another, when You have taken my heart from me?" Or I will say, "Here is my heart, take it from me. It is safer with you than with me."

> "I found him whom my soul loves; I held onto him and would not let him go." (Song of Solomon 3:4)

I will not let Him go. That's the picture of abiding. The definition of abiding means to *refuse to depart*. When Jesus tells us to abide in Him He is saying to *cling to Him*. It's not just so that wherever He is, there you are, but it is so that wherever He goes you will be dragged there with Him. *Cling to Him!*

Refusing to sin is far inferior to refusing to depart. He has not brought us into a life that merely says no to sin. He has brought us into a life in the Spirit in which the Bridegroom is blissfully enjoyed and we remain there. If you experience Him as He desires you to experience Him, your longings and cravings will be so satisfied that you'll look nowhere else. You'll be able to say with the psalmist, "The Lord is my Shepherd, I shall not *want.*" My wants are gone, vanished in the sight of You.

The reconciliation is God and man now finding their pleasure in one another. This is why Jesus split open the veil. His body was opened to bring you in so that you can enjoy what He is on the inside. You cannot eat a watermelon until it has been opened. So Jesus was opened on the tree to give you His internal contents to enjoy. Not merely enjoy, but through the enjoyment of eating Him, He becomes nutrients that give you His nature. Now you have a nourishment *from above* that gives you nutrients *from above* to walk out a life that is from *above*. This is why Jesus said such incredible things like, "I am the way." What was He saying? He knew that we would try to find a way and forget Him in the meantime, so He sewed Himself together with the phrase *the way*. He declared Himself to be *the way*.

In John 3:29, John the Baptist calls Jesus the Bridegroom. Then in Matthew 9:15, Jesus calls Himself the Bridegroom. The fact that this word Bridegroom is used to describe Him opens up an entire world of understanding. It brings an understanding of what He wants with you. If He named Himself chef, then you would know He wants to give you some food. Since He named Himself *bridegroom*, that means He wants to *marry* you.

I met a woman in Arizona once, who was so sweet. She had been through so much. She had been beaten, abused, and in bad relationships. She cried out to the Lord, "I want to get married Lord, but who will want me?" She heard the Lord speak behind her, "Marry me."

So I guess if there is any invitation, it is Jesus asking you to marry Him. What does that actually mean? It means giving Him all of your affection, let Him be first place, let His presence be the satisfaction to your soul where you look no longer for anything else.

"For I am jealous for you with a godly jealousy; for I betrothed you to one husband, so that to Christ I might present you as a pure virgin. But I am afraid that, as the serpent deceived Eve by his craftiness, your minds will be led astray from the simplicity and purity of devotion to Christ." (2 Corinthians 11:2-3)

Unless the simplicity and purity of the Bridegroom is experienced daily, your fire will go out. I've seen multitudes of people be powerfully touched by God. Yet when I saw them a few years later they're back on drugs, sleeping around, and living the opposite of devotion to the Lord. Why? Because the public touch didn't turn into a private kiss. Hudson Taylor said, "Many love Him truly, but not love Him *only*." Let our love be *only* for Him and not Him *and* all of the *additions*. In this, you'll wake up in the morning and your first thought is, "I want to be with You, Lord."

"Lord, when you came near, I could hear like the first sight of the blind,

like the redemption of all lost time.

Now you're more than home to me, and I'm left only with the memory of whoever I was before you passed by me.

Whenever I see you, near or far, I'm convicted of forgetting how beautiful you really are.

My heart is broken in two when it's kissed by You.

You melt away my ability to resist You, now my life consists of You.

As the grey light heralds the dawn, the sight of self is gone."

CHAPTER SEVEN
LOVING JESUS

"We are to come out of the King's chamber, pregnant with God's purposes."

You are the apple of God's eye; you are the treasure of this God of mine. No matter where you are in life, whether you're fantastic or awful, know this: He is head over heels for you. He wants to hear your voice, He loves when you turn your attention to Him. Simply doing so makes His heart race. If the inner life is anything, it is a life of being sick with love. Heralds that come forth from the King's chamber because those who have been so deeply touched and intimately kissed drip with God's fragrance. If the gospel is anything, let it be the fragrance of heaven.

The Bridegroom and the bride are not only symbolic of Christ and the church but Christ and the individual soul. When we see this wonderful, romantic, giddy, sweet, love exchange between Bridegroom and bride, we see God's intended and desired relationship with you and your heart. It is the clearest word picture in the scriptures of His racing love for you. Our inner life is to be baptized in *first love* and to have a heart racing for Him that makes His heart race.

In Song of Solomon, the entire romantic exchange between the bride and the groom is founded with and starts with, "Let him kiss me with the kisses of his mouth." This loving, intimate, direct contact with God is the experience of love. How do we know this? Because she goes on to say, "Your love is better than wine." These kisses of His love are what the scriptures are calling us into; to be directly contacted by God. We are to come out of the King's chamber, pregnant with God's purposes.

We must go forth from the King's chamber to find the lost and invite them to be loved by Him. The great emptiness inside of men is that they are missing Him. God's heart was so heavy with love for the lost that it dropped Him to the earth. When sin came in, man had forfeited God in his life, and the great hole in his heart is simply stated, "You are missing from me." God gathers men back to Himself not by demands, but by a demonstration of love on the cross forever unparalleled. God lacks a filter between His heart and His lips. He loves in kisses. What do I mean by that? I mean He longs to directly contact you intimately and lovingly, *repeatedly*. See, if we take experience out of our relationship with God, all we've got left is an idea. That experience is a sweet and tender kiss from God. Bernard of Clairvaux said, "The kiss is a participation in the life and love of the trinity. We are made one by this so we rest in rapture, which is the key of His mouth."

We, as blood-bought believers, have access to the sweet kiss of God, yet we often forget such things. Yet the lover in Song of Solomon, loves ardently because she is drunk with love. She is overcome by Him.

The kiss will keep us.

It thrills us and matures us. The bride looks for kisses before words.

The secret of the chamber with God: *look to be kissed before you even say anything*. Yet our closets are so plagued with words that we push out the kisses. Sometimes we forget how important it really is to receive the sweet nothings of God that satisfy our soul.

He is longing for those that will stare at Him and let the grin in His eyes linger inside of them. Who will look at Him, lean in, and be kissed? Kissed in such a way that whenever you lean out, you feel Him pulling you back in again. How do you know what the kiss is? I'll tell you this, the kiss is when you can feel in your heart the Holy Spirit saying something like this, "Don't leave. No, not yet. Stay with me."

Some of you reading this know exactly what I am referring to. Perhaps you felt it this morning in prayer, the sweetness was overtaking you and you felt as though God was holding you, pleading for you to stay with Him. The kiss can turn any location into a garden of spices with your Beloved. When He kisses you, He leaves gardens in your soul that reproduce after its own kind. He loves you and wants all of you. He sees that there are scars inside of each one of us, and only His kisses can heal them.

> His kiss is your call.
>
> His kiss is your cure.
>
> His kiss can cure my evil and bring me to His bliss, and give me Him for whom I sigh, Jesus my sweetness.

Sometimes you look around and say, "All this stuff is right in the midst of Christianity but something is missing."

Most of the time, what's *missing* is the *kissing*. There might be a lot of things, but there is no cure like God's kiss. Most of our issues can be solved right there. Most of the pain we experience in this life is the absence of the kiss. Whenever a friend comes to me for advice or counsel of any kind my first question is, when was your last kiss? *Lord, I was lost before your kiss, and now I'm lost without your kisses.*

It's possible to fall out of heights with God. It's possible to forget your first love like we see in Revelation 2. When you slip out of the kisses of God, you leave the heights with God. The scriptures say, "Whoever has ears to hear, let him hear," repeatedly. Specifically, in Revelation 2, Jesus declared this phrase after diagnosing a loss of first love. Having ears to hear simply means, *whoever will listen, will hear.* Those who take time to hear Him, will receive from Him. Whoever will not give Him attention will not hear the voice of His presence. If we don't give attention to His voice, then it's not going to be heard. And in this invitation itself to listen to Him and give him an ear, Jesus is already exposing the problem—a lack of attentiveness. The first love had been become second, third, fourth and beyond because of a lack of attentiveness.

Nothing else can jockey for position and rank within your heart. God won't share the throne of your heart with a theology, a practice, or a person. He wills to be unchallenged in your heart. Loving Jesus means that He holds your heart without competition. In Genesis 22, you see Abraham taking Isaac up onto the mountain. Everything

God had promised Abraham was housed in Isaac. Abraham's love was willing to kill all that God had promised him in order to obey Him. And God would rather kill all that He had promised Abraham if it meant Him losing first place in Abraham's heart. The angel stopped the process and spoke, "Now I know that you fear God" (Genesis 22:12). What a divine definition of the fear of God: *God unchallenged in the heart.*

When I was a young boy, my dad used to say to me, "I can see myself in your eyes." He'd look at me really close. The Lord brought it up to me one day and said it to me as my Heavenly Father, "I can see Myself in your eyes." With my own daughter, I looked at her and said the same thing. Then, she looked to the left. When she did, it dawned on me, *I could no longer see myself in her eyes.* I could only see myself in her eyes when she looked at me. God will only see Himself in *you* when you *look at Him.* If something else takes your attention away from Him, He won't see His character in you anymore.

The other day I was in prayer but I was all over the place. Some of you can relate. I was there, I was praying, yet I wasn't really looking at Him. I finally said, "What am I doing?" I stopped, looked up, and just said, "I worship You!" I felt like the Lord said, "There you are." You can teach it, yet forget it: adoration is the *key* to *see.*

CHAPTER EIGHT
LOVING JESUS
PART TWO

"It's possible to do His works and forget His face."

"TO THE ANGEL OF THE CHURCH IN EPHESUS WRITE: The One who holds the seven stars in His right hand, the One who walks among the seven golden lampstands, says this: 'I know your deeds and your toil and perseverance, and that you cannot tolerate evil men, and you put to the test those who call themselves apostles, and they are not, and you found them to be false; and you have perseverance and have endured for My name's sake, and have not grown weary. But I have this against you, that you have left your first love. Therefore remember from where you have fallen, and repent and do the deeds you did at first; or else I am coming to you and will remove your lampstand out of its place—unless you repent. Yet this you do have, that you hate the deeds of the Nicolaitans, which I also hate. He who has an ear, let him hear what the Spirit says to the churches. To him who overcomes, I will grant to eat of the tree of life which is in the Paradise of God." (Revelation 2:1-7)

If you could put Revelation 2:1-7 in a funnel, what would come out at the bottom? I believe this phrase from the mouth of Jesus: *love Me*. To this church, He said, "I know your deeds." What were they? First, He sees their *toil*. The word *toil* means perseverance even in the midst of pain. They were like spiritual marines, taking the beachhead for God. They stopped at nothing. Rain, sleet, or snow—they carried on.

Second, He notices their intolerance for sin. They dealt with sin immediately and didn't dabble in it. God honored their willingness to shun evil. They had discipline in this area.

Thirdly, their doctrine was so clean they knew who was false and who was not. They hated the religious system of *victory over the people*. Nicolatians was a combination of the word *nike* which is the greek word for *victory* and *ations* meaning *the people*. It taught hierarchy, separation, and the exaltation of man. They hated it and Christ complimented them.

Their duty, discipline and doctrine were all great. Yet the Lord was *still not receiving what He wanted from them*. Jesus was showing them, no matter how great these things are, they were not living an overcoming life. We think that our overcoming is in our discipline, duty and doctrine. We would think that a body of people like these, whose doctrine is clean, whose perseverance is strong and whose discipline is so uncompromising, were a victorious church. But Jesus shows that these folks had fallen from the heights of first love. They were missing the kissing. They had left the *first exchange of love*. Refusing to quit is far inferior to refusing to look away from Him. Refusing to sin is far inferior to refusing to depart from Jesus. Refusing error is far inferior to actually knowing Him.

Even when we have so many things that appear outwardly right, correct and in order—we can still be inwardly fallen. We think that fallen is defined by someone committing some sort of immorality yet Jesus thinks of falling in a different way. It's when He no longer has first place in the heart and when the mornings are not designated for Him who will illuminate the entire day. When He is no longer the one who is kissed, loved and adored, you have fallen.

We can hold onto our doctrine and still be fallen. We can hold onto our disciplines and still be fallen. We can hold onto our duty and still be fallen, from first love. I write these things to encourage you to love Him, to love the kisses, to look for kisses, to dive into kisses. He wants you to *swim* in the way that He makes you feel. If this language seems odd to you, let me explain it. People often want to separate *obedience* from *feeling*. The reality is, when you love, the nature of that love is obedience. If the life that we receive from Him is not greater than anything that can happen to us in this life, then it is inferior to it. But the life that He gives to us is so great that any greatness we experience in this life pales in comparison to the greatness of His life. You may have masses, miracles, money and the rest—but if He no longer has the heart, He isn't getting what He wants.

> "He who loves father or mother more than Me is not worthy of Me; and he who loves son or daughter more than Me is not worthy of Me." (Matthew 10:37)

This is first love. He is putting Himself as first priority and destroying all other loves. *I must be first,* is His heart cry. A love that does not cause a loss of self consciousness does not merit recognition. If love is still self conscious, He doesn't see it as real love. Real love is putting Him as first priority. Real love is God above me. Remember, Paul said that the man who is married is concerned about how to please his wife, and likewise the woman who is married is concerned about how to please her husband (see 1 Corinthians 7). This is a simple example of marital love for Jesus. If we are married to the Lord, our concern is pleasing Him, not pleasing ourselves.

The essence of our love is, "How can I please You, Lord? I want You to be pleased." It's not mere obedience, as a locker combination that pops open once you get it right. Praise God for obedience, but obedience that comes from love alone is pure! Obedience that is just to manipulate or make something happen is called feigned obedience. It's outward but not inward. There is a story of a little boy whose father told him to stand up. When he refused the father threatened the boy. When the boy stood to his feet he mumbled under his breath, "I am sitting on the inside." This is not the kind of obedience the Lord is looking for. He looks for a love from us that is so captivated by Him that self-renunciation our joy, if it means giving Him pleasure. These are the heights of first love.

> "He is also head of the body, the church; and He is the beginning, the firstborn from the dead, so that He Himself will come to have first place in everything." (Colossians 1:18)

This passage concludes that He is the head for the purpose of being first place in *everything*. He has put all things in place so that He could have first place, in everything. It's possible to do His works and forget His face. It has happened to so many people. The inner life of the believer should be blinded by the shining face of the Lord, looked at every single day.

> "No amount of activity in the King's service will make up for the neglect of the King." (G. Campbell Morgan)

> "All zeal for the Master that is not the outcome of the love relationship with Him is worthless." (G. Campbell Morgan)

It's the jealousy of the Bridegroom that burns like a flame and flashes like fire. Do you remember when you were first born again and you were so deeply in love with God and nothing would challenge Him? In fact you were offended when someone suggested that they could take God's place in any way. Nothing would keep you from spending time with Him. You saw everything that stood in between you and your prayer closet as a devil from hell. I'm telling you such a love shapes your value system.

Do you remember when hours felt like minutes? Do you remember when the entire Bible seemed to breathe? Do you remember when the sound of worship caused an eruption on the inside of you? The mere thought of being able to worship together with people was sheer joy. Do you remember when there was such an ease in His presence? There were difficulties and tribulations around, no doubt, but for some reason you just soared above them. These were the heights of first love.

Do you remember the sensitivity to the Spirit in the beginning? Do you remember the internal ache in your heart for God? Do you remember making meals for your family and weeping while you did? Washing dishes with dish soap and tears? Do you remember having to pull over while you drive to cry before the Lord?

God remembers these things. He longs for your return. He tells His people throughout scripture, "Remember!" His message is the same today. First love is what makes the heart of God so happy, because in it He gets exactly what He wants, which is to captivate your heart. His goal was never to corner men and collect their consent, but to captivate men's hearts.

Many want to take repentance out of the gospel, yet Jesus says, "Repent," to those who are saved. When you take repentance out of your life you burn the bridge that leads back to first love. Charles Spurgeon wrote, "See the secret of strength, look at Jesus and overcome. Let us lament our infrequent use of this conquering weapon. Now for a long and loving look at the Bridegroom of our hearts. Help us Holy Spirit, to whom we owe our sight." See, the eyes of the One that you love masters you. To live in the index of

His eyes is first love. The secret to overcoming, is being overcome by Him.

Having your doctrine perfect, your duty on point, and your discipline in tip top shape yet lacking first love is like a beautiful, gorgeous, decadent wedding without a groom. Listen, if you've lost this reality in your life in a daily way, I, with all the love in my heart, say to you, *remember the height from which you have fallen and turn back to gaze into His eyes so that He can see His image again.*

> "Tell me you're in the ocean and I'll walk into the sea, raise the waves of Your love and I'll let them bury me."

CHAPTER NINE

A CALL TO
LOVE
HIM

"Abandon your need to understand. Let His presence be more to you than answers and explanations."

"And the life was manifested, and we have seen and testify and proclaim to you the eternal life, which was with the Father and was manifested to us—what we have seen and heard we proclaim to you also, so that you too may have fellowship with us; and indeed our fellowship is with the Father." (1 John 1:2-3)

In closing this book, I want to encourage you to dive deep into this very fellowship. You could read all the books, spend all the time, and hear all the right teaching on fellowship with God yet the more you dive in the more you realize you haven't even begun to scratch the surface. May you dive deep into this inexhaustible Christ. Not only that, but may you call others into this very same reality. Let them know how blissful and beautiful He is. His presence is life itself and He is worth spending every drop of our energy, focus, life and blood on.

Toward the end of A.W. Tozer's life, he wrote something incredible: "When God sets out to really make a superior Christian, He is compelled to strip the man of everything that might serve as a false refuge, a secondary trust. He must shut the man up to Himself only." He is trying to strip you down to *naked trust.* God wills to take away every other crutch so that you lean wholly and completely upon Him.

May what was said of A.B. Simpson be said of you as well: "His enjoyment of the presence of the indwelling Christ almost literally transported Him. His was a ravaged heart which seemed to know no limit in its ardent devotion to the person of Jesus Christ."

Just before Leonard Ravenhill died, he said, "If we walk in the light as He is in the light, that's all that He asks of us; to walk in His light. I desire for you that you would all have more vision than I have ever had, more power than I have ever had, more understanding than I have ever had, and remember, no preacher ever had a bigger God, a bigger Bible or a bigger calendar than you do."

He went on to say, "Now in my final years, I have only one ambition, to get nearer to Jesus. I am determined this year, more than ever in my life, to know Jesus Christ in a new way, that I have not known Him yet before. I want to discover His majesty. I want to discover that glory that He had to the Father. Oh, there is a place of quiet rest near to the heart of God."

You have seen Him, you have heard Him, you have looked at Him with your eyes, you have touched Him with your hands; so from this place, allow Him to *save you everyday*. Allow it. He comes in like a knight in shining armor every morning to rescue you again. Don't resist Him. When He comes in to say, "Let me save you again today," don't say, "Nah, I've got it today."

Take your gaze away from yourself and look upon His beauty. It will melt away your ability to resist Him. Not only will it melt away your ability to resist Him but it will cause you to freely offer to Him the rights to your own life.

This is the byproduct of seeing how beautiful He truly is. I say to you, cling to Him, live by Him, love Him. I pray that you would burn for retreat with Him with a jealous desire that violently rejects even the smallest distractions.

Gladly let other desires die, that you may spend more time laying on His chest. Abandon your need to understand. Let His presence be more to you than answers and explanations. Seek refuge, seek strength, seek direction, seek grace under the divine shadow of this hidden secret place: the Man Christ Jesus. Depend utterly upon Him, so that it will be evident to all that you have become one with the One who said, "I can do nothing on my own initiative." Put yourself so deeply dependent upon Him that those who are stale and hollow will learn from your very life. What is it that your life should teach them? That *apart from Him we can do nothing.*

> "This is the kind of love that He deserves,
>
> So cherish His words,
>
> each letter, noun and verb—
>
> whispered or unheard.
>
> Vibrations and tremors,
>
> communications that enter
>
> the center of your being,
>
> Remember His feeding,

be tender to His leading,

see His heart bleeding,

For a harvest from the seeding of His Son.

The heeding of the one Gospel, that He made us to live in a life

that He died to give to His wife,

Marry Him daily,

and if failure should overtake thee,

may you see

that He is an advocate, sent from the Father

the kind and merciful potter,

now unto thee King, eternal, immortal, invincible, the only true and wise God, be all glory and honor and power and praise.

All to Him, all for Him, all by Him, and all through Him, the Bridegroom Himself."

Here are four signs of first love for Jesus. If any of these convict your heart, I call to you by the mercies of God to lay your heart at the feet of Jesus and sing, "Take my heart, take my whole life too. Cause I can't help falling in love with You."

1. No one and nothing captivates your heart like Him. You can be sure that if something else has more of a draw on your attention, Jesus doesn't have His proper place in your life.
2. Time with Him is more important than anything else. You refuse to not give Him time. It's not about a discipline. It's a pining. It's a longing. It's a coming away. If your prayer is driven by duty and discipline, look at the face of Jesus and you'll find that He is too beautiful to not look at. You will begin to throw yourself at His feet and His mercy again and again. Linking with Him won't be a chore but a delight. It's the secret of a sustained Christian life.
3. His Word means more to you than anyone else's words. Keith Green said, "My son, my son, my precious bride, the day is nearing when I'll take you in my arms and hold you. I know there are many things you've been hearing, but you just hold on to what I told you."
4. His desires mean more to you than your desires. When two become one flesh, you see the loss of self for the sake of another. That's marriage. And that's truly our union with the Lord.

I believe all of these things being sparked in your life are as simple as acknowledging that you need Him. If these things are not in your life, I invite you to bow your knee to the romantic King. Herein is the issue; will you bow your knee to the King? Will He become your *one and only?*

Pray this with me...

> "Here lies my heart,
>
> wicked, wounded, weary and in parts—
>
> deeply sank,
>
> blank.
>
> Redeem me again,
>
> esteem me Your friend.
>
> Lean in and mend
>
> my broken love.
>
> Cover me,
>
> take me up with Thee,
>
> Smother me
>
> to recovery,
>
> like there is no other but me,
>
> Let our eyes meet,
>
> as I lay on Your feet.
>
> Please keep me,

completely,

to finish from start,

heart upon heart.

Lord help me cling to You,

to sing to You,

to linger with You,

and bring to You everything I do!"

CHAPTER TEN

JESUS ALONE

A WORD FROM ERIC'S WIFE

"You can't love Him without Him."

THE MAJORITY OF CHRISTIANS TODAY HOLD THE NOTION that Jesus is not enough. They attend church regularly, attend all the conferences, read their bibles and pray. But deep down there's a dissatisfaction. They don't give too much attention to it because it's so easy to fill themselves with other things. They keep going to church, they keep praying, they keep on doing what they've been doing, never fully coming into the reality and fullness of what is available to them in their relationship with Jesus and what should be their "normal" Christian life. I can say these things because I was one of those people. I grew up in church. Church life was all I knew. We went on Sundays, youth group on Wednesdays and obviously we went on Easter and Christmas.

I used to stand there during praise and worship and the lyrics to the songs would be displayed on a huge screen for everyone to read and sing along. I would sing them and think, "I don't feel this way about God, where is this joy, where is this Healer?" I went to an Assemblies of God church so the worship was a bit more liberal than other denominations. There were people waving flags, raising their hands and dancing around. To me it was normal, sometimes a little weird, but it was all I knew. I began to question things.

I personally did not have any sort of connection to Jesus to experience things like unspeakable joy or peace that passes all understanding. I had a good life with good parents and even though things weren't perfect I was pretty content. I did feel conviction and I did believe in my heart that Jesus was real and He was the son of God and I did ask Him to come into my heart and be the Lord of my life. I believe I was saved. I read my bible and it always frustrated me and quite honestly bored me. I'm not really much of a reader to begin with but I knew reading the bible was something I just had to do. Because you know, I'm a Christian. But when I read it there were no deposits of life or explosions of joy on the inside due to the Holy Spirit revealing life changing truths in my spirit.

It was black and white, sometimes red words on a page going into my eyes. I was lucky if I remembered ANYTHING after reading it. I prayed. I prayed and I prayed. I asked for things, I prayed for God to protect my family and friends. I did a lot of talking. When I was done with my exhaustive list of requests I said, "In Jesus name Amen." Listen, I EVEN went to the Brownsville revival and experienced some of the craziest encounters with the Lord. I was filled with the Spirit and spoke in tongues. But even then, deep down inside, everything I did and said and believed was in hopes that it was all true. I did not have consistent fellowship with Jesus. What does that even mean? "Fellowship with Jesus." The definition of fellowship is friendly relationship; companionship. I did not have a friendly relationship with Jesus. I couldn't consider Him a companion. A companion is someone you are frequently in the company of. Was Jesus in my heart? Sure, yeah. Was He my best friend? No. Was He the lover of my soul? No. Was He the joy of my life? Definitely not. Was He enough? No.

I'm so grateful that I eventually came to terms with my dissatisfaction in Jesus. I began to say to Him, "Jesus I want to know you. The real you. The organic you. Strip away all the things that have been embedded in me that are not you. I just WANT to know who you are." I prayed this for years. I began to really see that I didn't really know Him. I struggled with condemnation and always feeling like I couldn't ever do enough. I felt like something was wrong with me because I wasn't in love with Jesus. I mean I was glad He came and died and I was thankful for all He had done for me, but when I said "I love you" it felt wrong because I wasn't sure I felt that way. How should it feel when you truly love Jesus? Is it like loving your family? You just automatically love them because they're your blood relatives?

Do you love Him like you love a friend? Do you love Him like you love your spouse? What does it even look and feel like when you love Jesus? I had all these questions and I truly wanted to be free from constantly feeling heavy and frustrated concerning Jesus, church and all things religious and/or spiritual. Being married to someone like Eric who prayed all the time and had this drive to always go away and pray and read the Bible was so weird to me. I always thought, "Ugh. I don't know how he does it. I'd go crazy." Eric understood intimacy with Jesus. He had come to know and love Jesus in a way I hadn't yet. I didn't really think I could get there, honestly, because I had zero grid in my own life for that kind of love for Jesus.

So how did I come to a place where I could say to you, and actually mean it, that Jesus is enough? Well, God began to answer the cry of my heart. When I talk to God I talk to Him very candidly and honest. He knows the core of our hearts anyway so there is no need to dress up your words. He wants your ugly. He wants your honesty. He wants EVERYTHING. The Lord brought people into our lives early in our marriage that truly loved Him, truly abided in Him and you could see it. I could see it in their demeanor, the way they talked about Him, the way they lived. It was intriguing to me. They were just normal people with their own unique personalities with families who were in love with Jesus. You see, I thought if you were a "sold out" Christian it should look a certain way and you would in some way lose your personality. Remember, I grew up in church, so I've seen it all. I had no desire to be or act like some of the Christians I had known or encountered. But these people were real and cool and funny. They were "normal" but different at the same time.

Through some of these relationships I began to learn that Jesus gave me my personality and it's OK. Some of you are probably thinking, "Well, duh." But I'm just telling you where I was and I have a feeling a lot of you reading this now are in the same place that I was; afraid to completely surrender to Jesus because you don't want to be one of the weirdos and be miserable because you're afraid you won't be happy. When I began to learn, or unlearn really, what it looked like to be a Christian, to be someone who loved Jesus, I began to talk to the Lord differently.

The real game changer for me was when I learned that I can't even love Jesus without Him. What I mean by that is, I thought I should just automatically love Him after learning about Him and knowing that He died for me. I thought it would be like me loving my family; it would just automatically happen. It doesn't. I never even thought of asking God to help me love Him because who does that? Is that even right? Would that be completely horrible of me to say, "Jesus I need you to help me love you because I don't love you enough." But that is exactly where freedom came for me. To realize that true love for Jesus comes from complete and utter dependency. Dependency is not weakness. Dependency IS Christianity. I need Him every second of every day. One of my favorite things Eric says in this book is:

> "We look to Him and live.
>
> When I stop looking at Him,
>
> I stop seeing Him.
>
> When I stop seeing Him,

I stop desiring Him.

When I stop desiring Him,

I start looking for other things."

That is such a short, easy, but profound way to explain the Christian life. He is everything. He is enough. When you start to deal with the dissatisfaction in your own heart and begin to ask Jesus to help you love Him you will begin to see Him and then you will love Him. This love is like no other love. It's beyond love for family. It's beyond love for friends. It's beyond love for your spouse. I can't really describe it. It's a love that is so fulfilling, so full of life, so full of love and joy. It's freedom. It's Jesus. He's so good. He's so real. He's so alive.

There is so much more available to you as a believer and follower of Jesus. Don't settle for dead religion. Don't settle for traditions. When you read this book open your hearts and be real with the Lord and with yourself. We all have to face the things that are in our own hearts. No one is exempt from that. This book is a simple, straight to the heart explanation of what all of us as believers should be experiencing in our daily lives as we daily abide in Jesus and daily come to the table and eat of Him. Just as you couldn't survive your natural life if you didn't eat food, you cannot survive your spiritual life without eating Him. He is your bread from heaven.

He is your SOURCE OF LIFE. You can't love Him without

Him. Don't complicate it. Tell Him you need Him. Tell Him you need Him to help you love Him and then let Him do it. The joy really is real. Jesus really is real. He really can fulfill you. He really can set you free. He really can provide. He really can love you and in turn you really can love Him.

MEET THE AUTHOR

Eric William Gilmour is the founder of *Sonship International*—a ministry seeking to bring the church into a deeper experience of God's presence in their daily lives. He enjoys writing on the revelation of Jesus Christ in the Scriptures and personal experience of God. He lives in Florida with his wife Brooke and their two daughters.

DISCOVER MORE AT:

sonship-international.org

ALSO BY ERIC

Sonship: Essential Writings from Eric Gilmour

Honey

Naked Trust

Mary of Bethany

Burn

Lovesick

Union

Into the Cloud

How to Prosper in Everything

How to Be Happy

Enjoying the Gospel

Divine Life

The School of His Presence

Nostalgia

*ALL TITLES AVAILABLE AT **AMAZON.COM**

MAXIMS

"Above all, be faithful to the present moment, which will bring you all needful grace."

—Fenelon

"In the lover's life, giving time to the one you love is not a matter of discipline but jealousy."

"The same devil that pushes one towards pornography pushes another towards self purgation. We must live dependent upon the Spirit to remain in His person and not grieve Him by either of these evils."

"Frustrations invite staleness."

"Jesus as everything is not a minimalist life. Jesus as everything is an endless supply."

"To be a bit more conscious of the warm, living, loving presence of my Jesus, I knelt by the bed to pray."

—Ruth Paxson *(alone in a guest house on a ministry trip)*

"I can't think of a higher prize than His eyes."

"Absolutely nothing is as insidiously poisonous as spiritual pride. It is fostered by what seem to be the most humble practices. The real, life-giving, daily experience of Jesus is the only way to learn humility."

"Some of us have cried out for revival and forgotten to tell Jesus that we love Him."

—Michael Koulianos

"Grumbling is often fostered by logic. Listening>Logic."

"An imaginary Christ gives an imaginary salvation."

—The early church dealing with heresies

"Anyone who thinks that beholding Christ is unnecessary to Christian practice and sanctification does not know Christ, nor the gospel."

—John Owen

"Holiness is exclusive love."

"Don't look for something. Look at Him."

"The only way for Jesus to be our supreme desire is for us to give up to Him every one of our other desires."

"Even obedience is inferior to Jesus."

"Many Christians have wings but cannot fly into the heights of first love because of the weight of their self-consciousness."

"Where your treasure is, there your heart will be also. If He is our treasure, our hearts will be His."

"To preach Him is very different to preaching about Him, even though His person be the theme."

—Penn-Lewis

"He that loveth not, looketh not."

"...Naked is the path of faith."

—Guyon

"Let's give more attention to Jesus as truth than to the truths of Jesus."

"The fact that truth is a Person means that it could never be separated from sensible experience."

"To give your affection to Jesus means nothing is competing with Him for your attention."

"He loves you with all your scars. So love Him right where you are."

"We are not looking for a mere feeling, we are looking at Jesus. But when Jesus is seen, He is the height of all feelings."

"To master my will, He had to melt my heart."

—Ruth Paxson

"Attend more to humbling your spirit, than to upholding your opinion even when it is right."

—Fenelon

"He alone is from above. Therefore, every single

thing that doesn't issue out of a love that yields itself to Him is from below."

"I found that it was Himself coming in, instead of giving what I needed."

—A.B.Simpson

"Friends, our trouble is the absence of ecstasy."

—Tozer

"The gospel is from heaven and it can only bring that which is in keeping with heaven."

"When Paul saw the beauty of Jesus his response was, '...I went away...'"

—Galatians 1:16-17

"He waits to be wanted."

—Tozer

"I think one of the main reasons Adam ate from the tree of the knowledge of good and evil is because the tree of Life didn't have all his attention."

"...I am a nobody."

—Paul The Apostle, 2 Corinthians 12:11

"My hero is a woman who never preached a sermon, wrote a book or performed a miracle. She simply recognized, cherished and loved Jesus above herself and everybody else."

"Only if He is everything can He safely give us anything."

"Our ministry is the expression of our enjoyment of the Lord."

"His presence is certain security and supply, always, and for everything."

—H.W. Smith

"God was waiting in the depth of my being to talk with me if I would only get still enough to hear Him."

—A.B. Simpson

"Before He can perform it through you, He must detach it from you."

"When you choose not to give your attention to His presence you are choosing not to have joy unspeakable and peace that passes all understanding."

"Enjoying Jesus is the only way to become like Him. It is finding everything in Him that makes us like Him."

"Don't trust any leading that comes before satisfaction with His person."

"The most important daily habit we can possess is to remind ourselves of the gospel."

—Spurgeon

"We have no problem believing that salvation is by grace and not our works but can't seem to believe the Christian life is also by grace and not our works."

"Never let the route or arrival take your attention from The Cloud."

"The lower you are, the more there is. The higher you go, you're only His."

"God's commands to us are actually given to the life of His Son within us."

—Oswald Chambers

"So many people are trying to experience Jesus and fail to realize that being attentive to Jesus is the experience. Upton said, 'I get so thirsty trying to find Your presence that I forget to stop and just take a drink.'"

"We cannot win the world until He has won our hearts."

"The voluntary giving up of all the rights of our lives can only be a result of beholding His beauty."

"Quiet solitude is avoided by most of us simply because silence before God exposes how hollow, scattered and self reliant we are."

"You know when you know your identity? When you forget about it."

—Michael Koulianos

"The heart that praises God cannot be sad."

—Carlos Annacondia

"You know what makes a bad worship leader? Someone who doesn't believe that God is worthy."

—Jeremy Riddle

"What if the only limitation to our experience of

the goodness of God is what we are willing to believe of His goodness?"

"May we never let our lack of experience define God's character."

"Faith is the submission of the mind. Whatever actions do not issue from faith are sin."

"The prideful can pray but only those who humble themselves can communion."

"Some rest in order to gain power for work, others find rest to be the power of their work."

"Prayer is the bleeding of the heart. Preaching is the overflow of the life. Worship is the giving up of one's soul."

—Paul Ravenhill

"Ocean depth of happy rest."

—Beethoven on God

"It is thought that Spiritual maturity is less need to sense God and more need to understand God. True maturity is rather more ability to sense God and less need to understand God."

"Some Christians are so dependent upon their own disciplines that if the Holy Spirit left them their life would look exactly the same as it did before."

"Only what we relinquish to Him can He be for us."

"There is no part of Christianity whatsoever meant to be accomplished without the real, living and interactive power and person of the Holy Spirit. He must be the lens through which every single thing is viewed or we miss the New Covenant completely."

"The life of faith means never knowing where you are being led. But it does mean loving and knowing the One who is leading."

—Chambers

"The indwelling presence is the focal point of prayer."

—Teresa of Avila

"Every time you sit with God the course of your life changes."

"Evil has no beginning but pride."

—Andrew Murray

"My daughter read to me tonight. 'I am not looking for someone perfect. I am just looking for someone to love with all my heart.'"

"There exists no pain so sharp as realizing I have given the attention He deserves to something far inferior to Him."

"One can peel a potato to the glory of God if he looks full in the face of Jesus."

"We cannot muscle ourselves into His image we can only yield to the Spirit's nature."

"The highest moments in your life will be when you are alone in worship and adoration. These will surpass all the preaching you ever heard in your life."

—Ravenhill

"When you enjoy Him, everything He puts in you is delightful."

—K.Walters

"We must entertain ourselves from day to day with the contemplation of the beauty of the Lord."

—Matthew Henry

"If we do not value satisfaction in prayer we end up elevating the discipline of prayer."

—Michael Koulianos

"You have captured my heart; taken it from me. Keep it Lord. It is safer with You than me."

"To compare myself with others would mean that I do not find everything I need in Him."

"Prayer is simply sustaining the sweet sense of His person."

"Competition is evil and prideful. Any activity that springs from it cannot please God. No matter the results. Humility prefers others and all that springs from it is pleasing to God. No matter the results. Don't try to do something "better," just do what God has said."

"Everything is found in Him. The moment we actually believe that, all the other tiresome pursuits will end."

"We will never get back the time we waste trying to be noticed."

"The fear of missing His call must be greater than

the fear of failing."

—Daniel Kolenda

"The greatest thing that can happen to you today is the loss of self adoring Jesus."

"Love hands over and takes captive all other forms of affection. That is why one who loves knows nothing else."

—Bernard of Clairvaux, The Song of Songs

"Nothing is so imperfect as being impatient with the imperfections of others."

"The Spirit was sent to get it all out of the book and into my life."

"Do not be disheartened by your falls. Inasmuch as they clearly point out your weak places, they ought to make you more humble, and more diligent to abide in constant recourse to God as a means of preservation."

—Fenelon

"Once you have quieted your heart and set your affection upon Him in adoration—it is important that you are void of any intent to move on. Just rest.

Enjoy. Smile in His goodness and let gratitude and love continually rise up from your heart to His."

"Patience is what attentiveness to God looks like."

"Waiting is the sustained exclusion of all other things."

"Christian perfection has not the strictness, the irksomeness, the constraint that some imagine. It requires that we should be devoted to God from the depths of our heart and when we are thus devoted to him all that we do for him becomes easy."

—Fenelon

"Strip away all the things I can do for you.

Strip away all the things I've done for you.

Strip away all the things I want from you.

Strip away all the things I need from you.

Strip me to naked love for you."

"The more peaceful and trusting you remain, the more rapidly you will advance because self energy will not obstruct you. Take care, dear one, to direct your attention toward God."

—Guyon

NOTES

NOTES

NOTES

NOTES

Printed in Great Britain
by Amazon